The Best Advanced
PAPER
AIRCRAFT

Long Distance Gliders, Performance Paper Planes,
and Gliders with Landing Gear

Carmel D. Morris

First published by Angus & Robertson, 1983

Reprinted several times by Angus & Robertson, Harper Collins, Putnam NY,
and Big One Productions

This edition Copyright 2023, Big One Productions

ISBN: 978-1466402461

Cover design: Big One Productions

Editor: Sandra Thompson

Line drawings: C. Morris

Typeset in Palatino Linotype 11pt

This edition is printed in the United States of America

10 9 8 7 6

Preface

This book is written by a best-selling author of over 35 books including *Paper Boats!* (Harper Collins), *Paper Spacecraft* (Scholastic), and *Paper Airplanes in Cardboard*, (Scholastic, Big One).

There are some unique designs by Carmel that many over the years have tried to copy in their books; this book was first published when Carmel was a teenager; the models she designed while still at school which proved useful for many students in school assemblies and college.

Recalcitrant by nature, Carmel found fame amongst her college peers and these books became international best sellers almost overnight. Many origami paper aircraft book authors were inspired by her books and in the *Best Paper Aircraft* tradition wrote their own books – but this book started it all for more complicated paper aircraft. This book has also been known to have inspired many young people into engineering and scientific fields. It is often used for education in schools, colleges and exhibits; the Dallas Love Field *Frontiers of Flight Museum* paper plane training is a fine example.

Now I am happy to release this book for a new generation of keen paper airplane folders. There's a model to suit every occasion, from the historical to modern, performance and wind-catchers, to long distance gliding, and every aerobatic style in-between.

Happy folding and flying!

Col. Dwight Edwards (Retired)

Contents

Introduction

Welcome to the fun world of paper airplanes. Not just your average dart, *The Best Advanced Paper Aircraft* will show you how to fold and fly some amazing models. Most of the models in this book are folded; you do not have to cut anywhere but for rear tail lift in some models, and shaping a wing section in the WWI Fokker.

About the paper sizes

All models in this book are made from standard US Letter which also works well for A4, despite a slightly different aspect ratio.

Ensure paper weight is in the range of 80 to 100 gsm (grams per square meter). This ensures good rigidity in folds, i.e. better creases. Do not use paper that is thicker, since more complicated folds can come undone. *Photocopy paper is ideal*.

Folding

In this new edition, base folds are repeated for each model that uses them and the more difficult folds are accompanied with photographs.

Always remember safety; do not throw your darts in the direction of people. Pointed objects could hit an eye.

If any glider dives, add some tail lift on the trailing edges by curling up the paper. For advice on good folding practice and throwing, *Paper Plane Throwing Tips* is now available.

Folding Techniques

Symbols

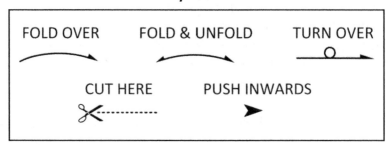

FOLD OVER   FOLD & UNFOLD   TURN OVER

CUT HERE   PUSH INWARDS

Techniques

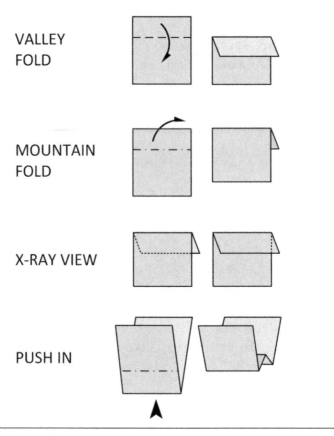

VALLEY
FOLD

MOUNTAIN
FOLD

X-RAY VIEW

PUSH IN

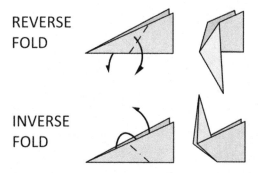

REVERSE FOLD

INVERSE FOLD

Rabbit Ear Fold

Make a diagonal crease-fold, and then two intersecting crease-folds. Bring in the sides and pinch together to form a point, and then flatten the point.

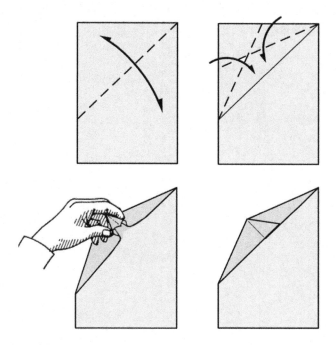

Long Distance Glider 1

If you are sitting way at the back of a lecture theater or cinema and do not find it entertaining, this dart will get your message across!

1 Long Distance MK1

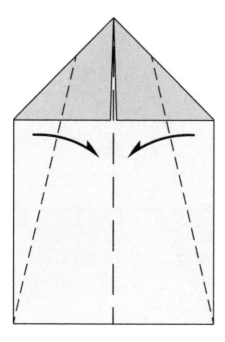

In Step 1, begin with a sheet of paper crease-folded in half and the top corners folded in. Fold the side corners in to meet the center crease.

2 Long Distance MK1

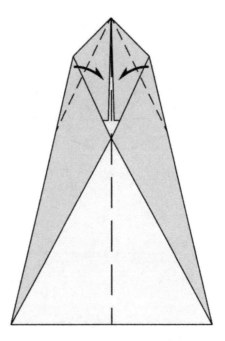

Fold the top corners in to meet the center crease (the top angled edges will meet and align to the center crease).

3 Long Distance MK1

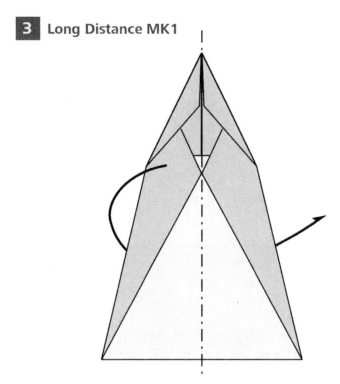

Fold behind lengthwise in half.

4 Long Distance MK1

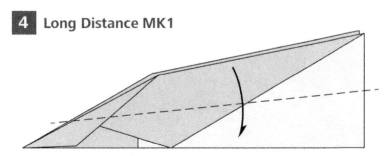

Fold the wings down and keep them level.

5 Long Distance MK1

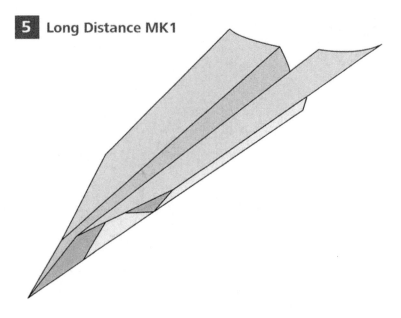

Your dart is now complete. Curl the tail section slightly upwards for lift if you need it. If the model stalls, reverse fold back the nose by an inch or so.

Throw with gentle force at approximately 30 to 40 degrees in an upward direction. Because of its length, this dart will prove accurate in meeting its target.

Super Wing

This is an incredible performance paper wing. It is surprisingly stable as a glider and can perform some aerial manoeuvres too.

1 Super Wing

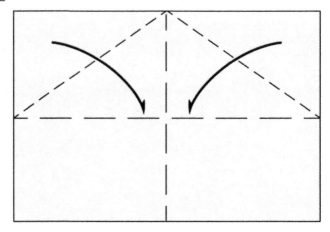

Begin with a sheet of paper facing you horizontally and crease-folded in half in both directions along the dashes.

Now fold in the corners from where the creases start on the paper edges.

2 Super Wing

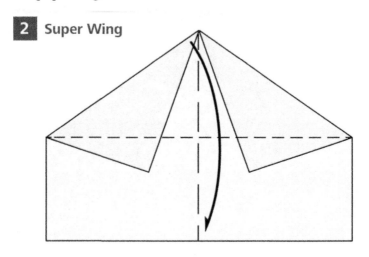

3 Super Wing

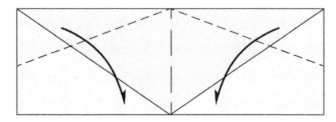

4 Super Wing

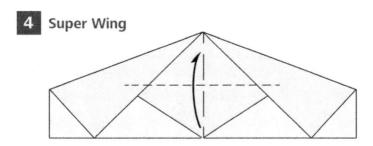

In Step 4, fold point up to nose, tucking under the outer flaps.

5 Super Wing

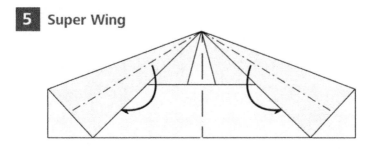

In Step 5, fold back the flaps along the dots and dashes (mountain fold) to strengthen the leading edge.

6 Super Wing

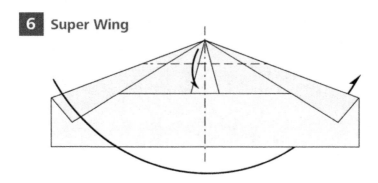

In Step 6, fold nose down, and then fold behind in half. Rotate model to face you as shown in Step 7.

7 Super Wing

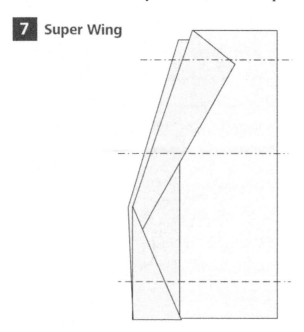

In Step 7, where the valley fold is indicated, fold the wings down; where the mountain folds are indicated, fold wing fins back.

8 Super Wing

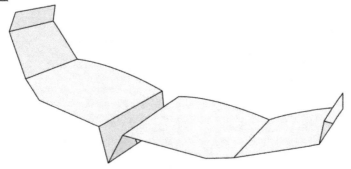

The completed Super Wing. Throw horizontally with slight force. If your model is perfectly symmetrical, it should be able to perform loops when thrown with greater force in an upward 45 degree angle.

To make the Super Wing return to you in a relative horizontal circle, throw it upwards and away from you at approximately 30 degrees with its underside facing you.

Long Distance Glider MKII

Here is a dart that can be thrown with greater force due to its solidly-constructed nose section.

While staying at the Hotel del Coronado in San Diego, we snuck into the red-roofed turret to have a look. On the lookout above we were able to throw these and they stayed aloft, sailing across the ocean air, coming to land (we presumed) at the naval base next door, as it had flown off in that direction. We hope they made a good touchdown on a carrier!

1

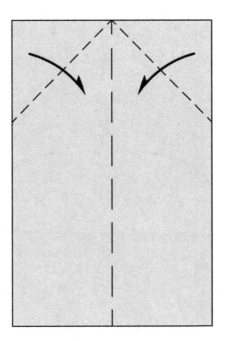

Begin with paper crease-folded lengthwise in half, and then fold the corners in as for a regular dart.

2 Long Distance MK2

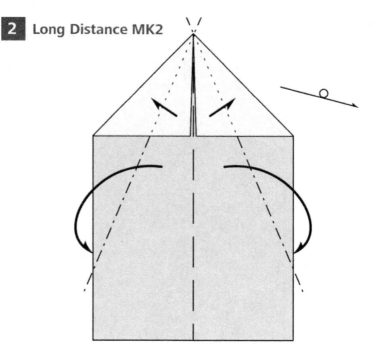

In Step 2, as you fold the sides behind (including the hidden section (dotted line), the top corners flip out and go around behind. Next, turn the paper over (arrow symbol with circle).

3 Long Distance MK2

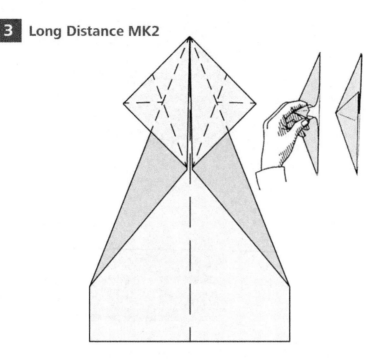

In Step 3, we will make 'rabbit ears' on the top sections. To do this, make crease-folds and then pinch the edges together to make an 'ear' section on each side.

The following photos may help...

4 Long Distance MK2

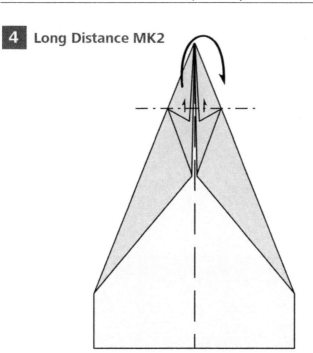

In Step 4, fold the nose behind and flip forward the two bunny 'ears'.

5 **Long Distance MK2**

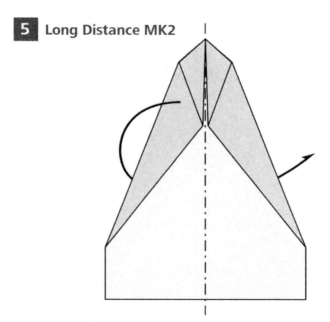

6 **Long Distance MK2**

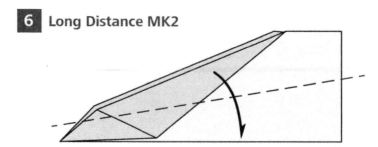

7 Long Distance MK2

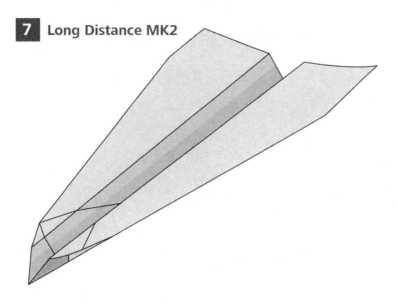

The completed glider; curl up the tail section slightly if you need extra lift. Throw upwards with moderate force, preferably against or slightly side-on to the wind.

Megadart (Super Dart)

This popular model has been used in several books and cell phone apps, including our own *Paper Aircraft Advanced* Apple and Android app.

1 **Megadart**

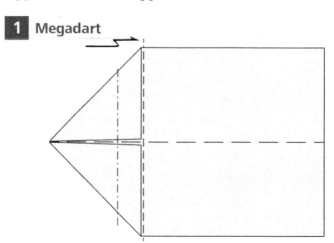

Make a 'stair-step' fold: where indicated, valley-fold to the right, and then back to the left.

2 Megadart

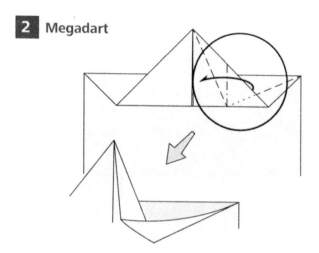

In Step 2, make creases and place finger under right-hand section, and then pull to the left. Repeat for the left side, and flip the model around to that shown in Step 3.

3 Megadart

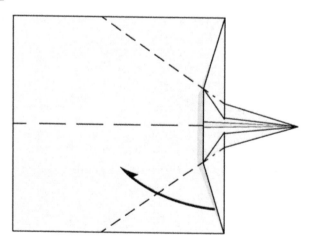

In Step 3, make creases and 'inverse' fold this section, turning the corner folds inside out and towards the center crease.

4 Megadart

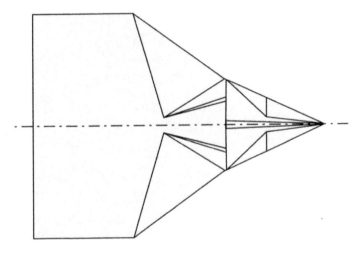

5 Megadart

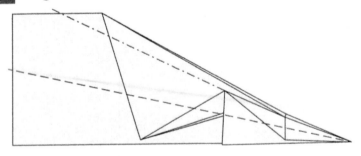

Fold the side fins inwards, starting from the back of the nose cone section. Next, fold down the wings.

6 Megadart

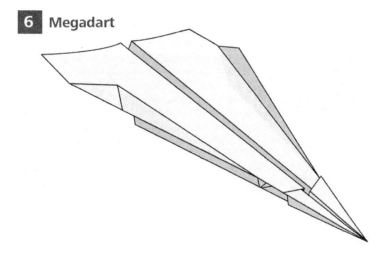

The completed craft is now ready to fly. Curl up the tail section slightly if you require more lift.

Throw hard and high. With the nose section tilted slightly, you should be able to get a decent-sized loop. Try making this model using stiffer paper; it will last longer.

Super Looper (Original Ninja)

Many authors have copied this model with slight variation to get around copyright but the result is poorer performance. This is the original and best design for outstanding looping performance.

This craft begins with a standard basic fold. In step 1 you will see diagonals (valley folds). The horizontal dot-dash (mountain fold) line means you crease behind. This allows you to bring the sides together and collapse the paper to make the basic fold.

Let's try it now…

1 **Super Looper**

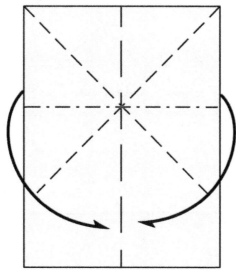

In Step 1, make all creases (the horizontal is folded behind) and then unfold. Now bring in the sides and collapse down the top as shown in Steps 2 and 3.

2 **Super Looper**

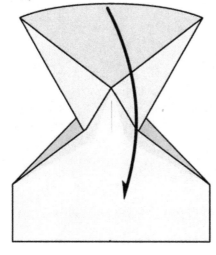

3 **Super Looper**

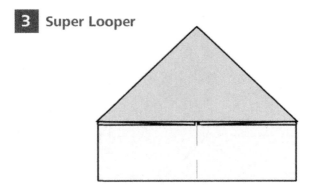

Step 3 shows the finished basic fold. If you have difficulty with this fold, the following photos may assist.

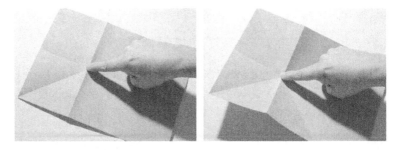

Pushing in the center will pop up the sides.

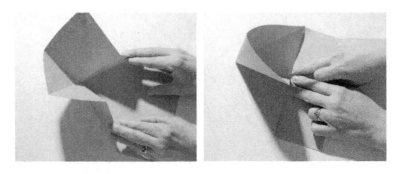

You can then collapse the sides together to make the new fold.

4 Super Looper

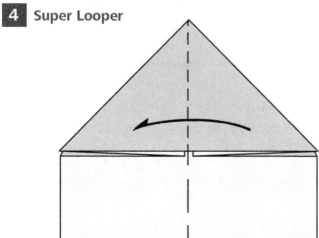

Swing the upper right flap to the left.

5 Super Looper

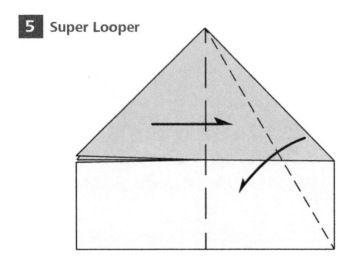

Fold the side in from nose to bottom right corner. Next, flip back to the right the upper left flap. Repeat Steps 4 and 5 for the other side.

6 Super Looper

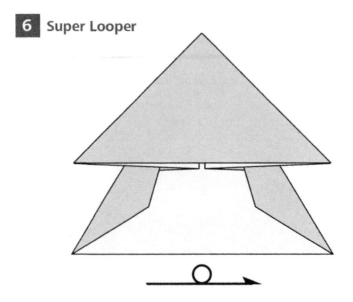

Turn the model over.

7 Super Looper

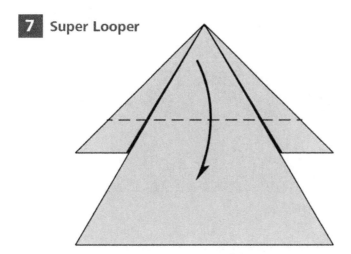

Fold nose down.

8 Super Looper

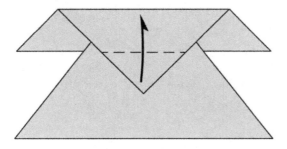

Fold back up; this will create solid fuselage for you to grip for throwing.

9 Super Looper

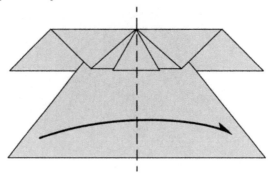

Fold in half and swing the model about to face you for Step 10.

10 Super Looper

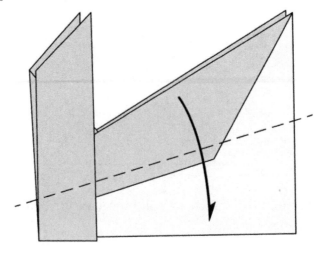

Fold down wings, and keep them relatively level.

11 Super Looper

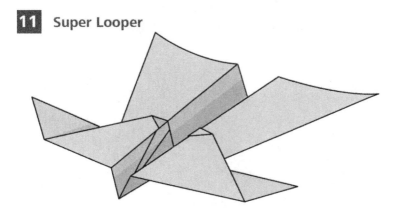

The completed Super Looper; throw upwards with force and it will do a big loop. If thrown at the wind, it will be picked up and carried away. Adjust the amount of tail curl (more trailing edge upward curl for indoors, meaning a smaller diameter loop so you don't hit the ceiling). This model is ideal for halls etc.

There is a video of this on Dwight's YouTube channel, **Paper Plane Lab**.

WWI Fokker Eindecker

This early monoplane (1915) is not only a novelty, but flyable! If the lesson is Aviation History, show your appreciation by landing one of these on the teacher's desk.

It is recommended to cut an inch off the long edge of the paper for a longer aspect ratio. While the model flies well using A4 or Letter paper, a longer fuselage will provide better stability.

1 WWI Fokker Eindecker

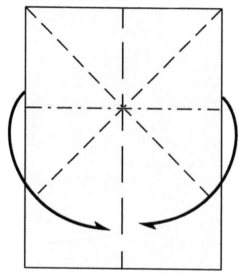

In Step 1, 2 and 3, crease and make a basic fold, same as for Super Looper.

2 WWI Fokker Eindecker

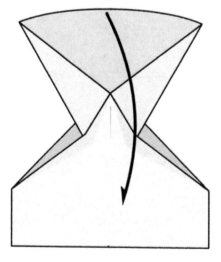

3 WWI Fokker Eindecker

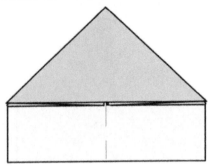

This is the finished basic fold.

4 WWI Fokker Eindecker

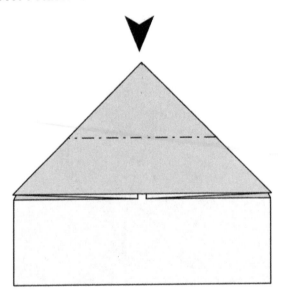

Crease well on all sides and push the point inwards by opening out the fold, pushing in the center, and then collapsing it all again.

5 WWI Fokker Eindecker

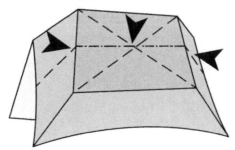

This shows the opened out fold.

6 WWI Fokker Eindecker

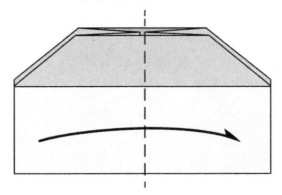

Fold in half the entire model.

7 WWI Fokker Eindecker

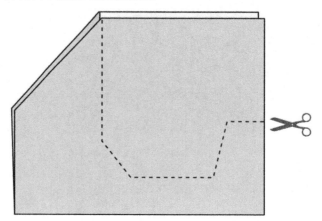

Cut off the unwanted area to make a wing shape.

8 WWI Fokker Eindecker

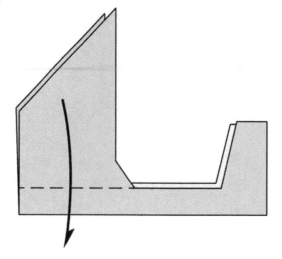

Fold the wing down. In the following steps we will make the undercarriage.

9 WWI Fokker Eindecker

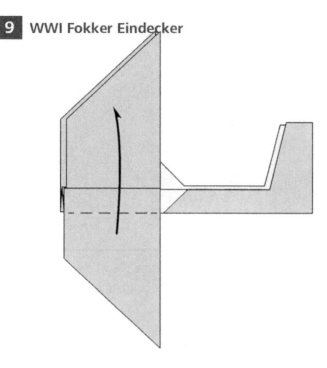

Fold back up along bottom edge of fuselage.

10 WWI Fokker Eindecker

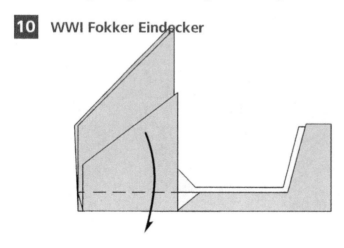

Fold down again.

11 WWI Fokker Eindecker

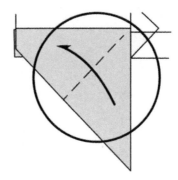

Steps 11 – 14 show a cutaway section detailing the landing gear assembly for one side. When done, repeat for the other side.

12 WWI Fokker Eindecker

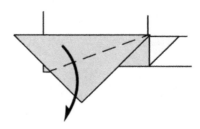

13 WWI Fokker Eindecker

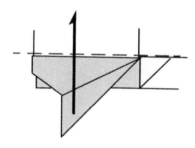

Swing up the leg.

14 WWI Fokker Eindecker

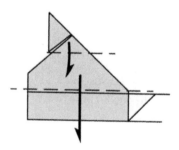

Fold top point to lock the leg, and then swing the section down.

15 WWI Fokker Eindecker

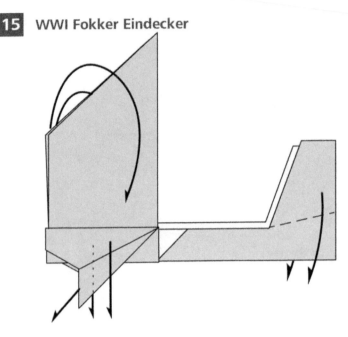

Swing the wings down to horizontal, grasping each end at the tips and pulling gently to straighten the wingspan. Lower the undercarriage to support the plane. Fold the tail wings down and you are now ready to fly.

16 WWI Fokker Eindecker

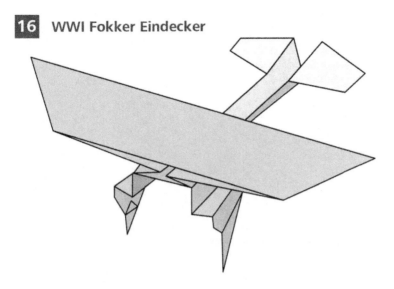

This finished WWI craft is more of a gentle flier than the original which turned the British aircraft into 'Fokker fodder' during World War 1.

Place your index finger inside the fuselage at the tail section while grasping the underside of the fuselage with thumb and forefinger. With a slight downward movement, gently let go of your craft. It will glide to a soft landing.

Glider with Landing Gear

Lands well on a desk! The undercarriage also provides stability. The undercarriage design is more refined than the WWI aircraft and can be used in that plane also.

The craft uses the same basic fold as the Super Looper, and the base fold steps are repeated for your convenience.

1 Glider with Landing Gear

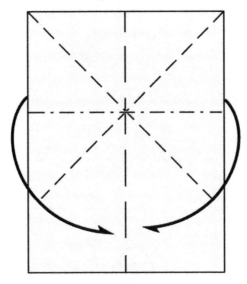

2 Glider with Landing Gear

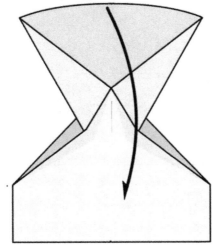

3 Glider with Landing Gear

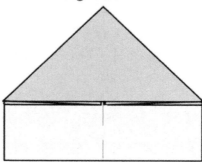

The finished basic fold.

4 Glider with Landing Gear

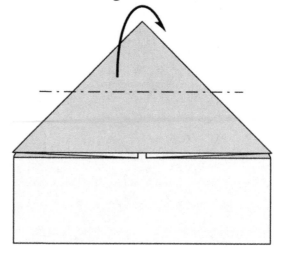

Fold nose section behind.

5 **Glider with Landing Gear**

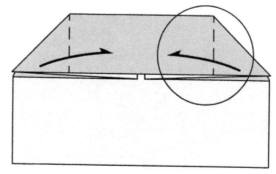

In Steps 5 – 12 we will make the undercarriage. Fold upper flap corners in towards center.

6 **Glider with Landing Gear**

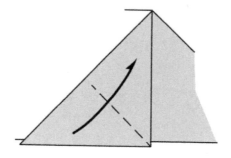

This is a close-up view of the right-hand undercarriage.

7 **Glider with Landing Gear**

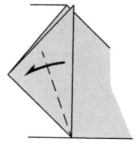

8 Glider with Landing Gear

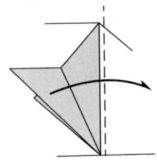

Swing to the right.

9 Glider with Landing Gear

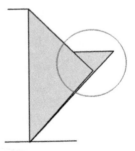

Let's take a closer look at the 'wheel' section…

10 **Glider with Landing Gear**

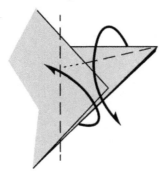

Step 10 shows a close-up cutaway of the landing feet detail. As you fold the triangle section to the left, fold the upper horizontal edge down. Step 11 shows this process under way.

11 **Glider with Landing Gear**

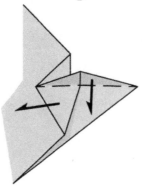

Flatten the fold when done, and repeat for the other side.

12 Glider with Landing Gear

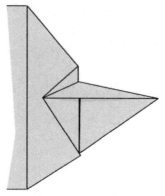

Done! If you wish to square-off the 'wheel', fold the right point to the left by a quarter inch or so.

Repeat for the other side.

13 Glider with Landing Gear

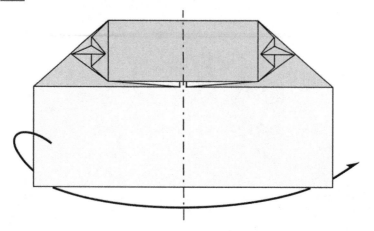

Fold in half behind.

14   Glider with Landing Gear

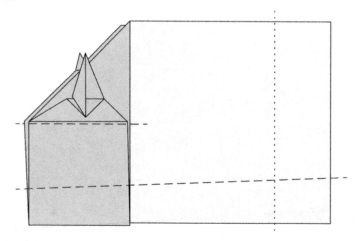

In Step 14, fold wings and undercarriage down. If your glider stalls, cut the trailing edge back around half an inch.

15   Glider with Landing Gear

Throw horizontally away from you towards a smooth surface and watch it land gracefully.

Dive Bomber MK1

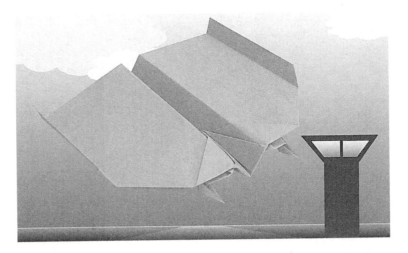

This craft is a neat dive bomber when thrown hard and down towards a target.

Also known as a sea plane (though there is a better one in the *Paper Boats!* book), this craft can actually float somewhat in water if the undercarriage is bowed out and the craft is folded using plastic sheeting/wrapping paper.

This model uses the same basic fold as the Super Looper, and base fold steps are repeated here for your convenience.

1 Dive Bomber 1

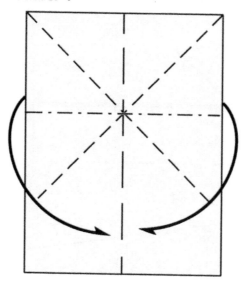

2 Dive Bomber 1

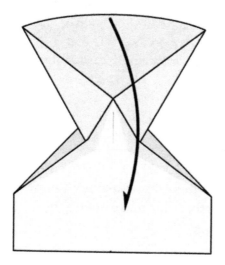

3 **Dive Bomber 1**

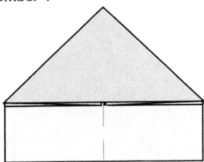

The finished basic fold.

4 **Dive Bomber 1**

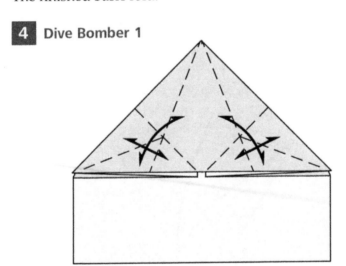

Larger view; in this step, make all the creases and pinch the sides together to make two big bunny ears, by following Steps 5 – 7.

5 **Dive Bomber 1**

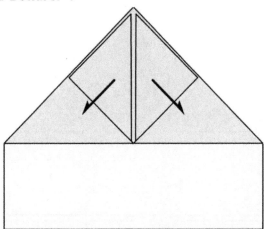

6 **Dive Bomber 1**

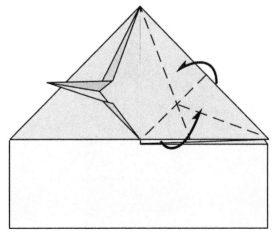

7 **Dive Bomber 1**

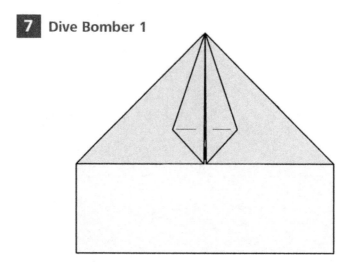

How it should look.

8 **Dive Bomber 1**

Fold upper right-hand point down and to the right.

9 Dive Bomber 1

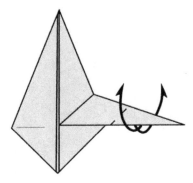

In Step 9, make a diagonal crease, put your finger inside the flap and then 'reverse' the fold (opening it and turning it inside out).

10 Dive Bomber 1

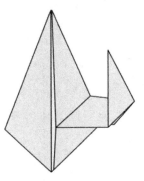

In Step 10, repeat this fold for the left side.

11 **Dive Bomber 1**

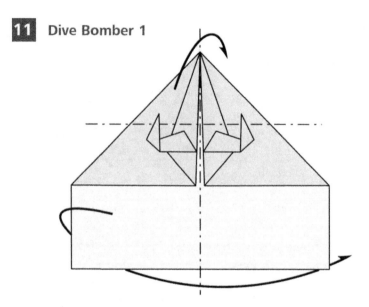

In Step 11, Fold nose section behind and then fold the model in half behind.

12 **Dive Bomber 1**

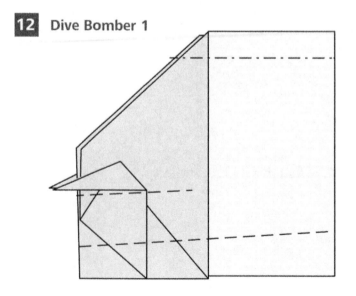

In Step 12, fold down the 'guns' with the wings, otherwise fold them downwards and open out the legs to make skis if you want to make a 'water landing' craft.

13 **Dive Bomber 1**

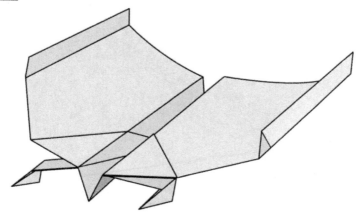

The completed diver bomber; if the craft stalls, trim off the trailing edge wing section by around half an inch.

Shuttle Copter

This thing can be thrown hard and high into the air, yet it spins gently down, somewhat reminiscent of a pine cone seed.

This model uses the same basic fold as the Super Looper, and base fold steps are repeated here for your convenience.

1 Shuttle Copter

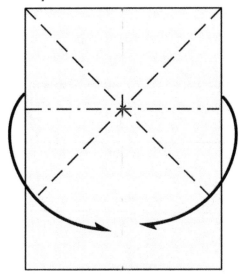

2 Shuttle Copter

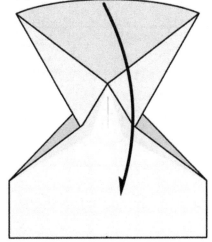

3 **Shuttle Copter**

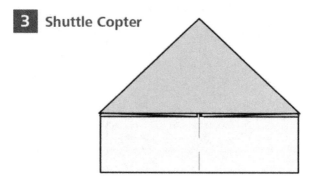

The finished basic fold.

4 **Shuttle Copter**

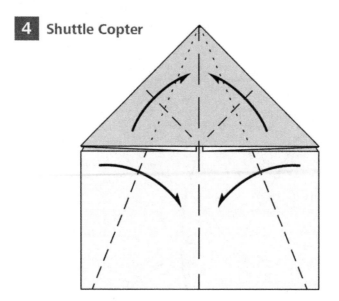

Fold top triangle flaps up and fold sides in to the center, under the top flaps.

5 **Shuttle Copter**

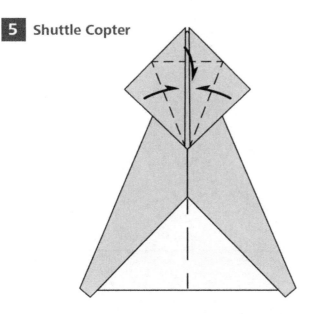

In Step 5, fold upper sides in and tuck their corners into the top section as you fold it down.

6 **Shuttle Copter**

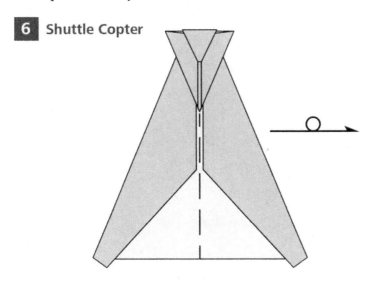

7 Shuttle Copter

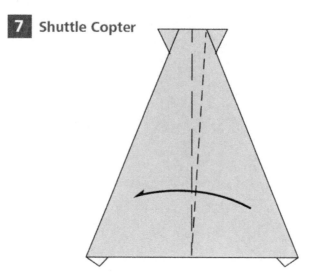

Fold right-hand wing to the left. Be careful not to go past the model's center crease.

8 Shuttle Copter

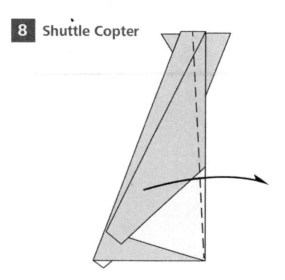

Fold back again, and repeat for the left side.

9 **Shuttle Copter**

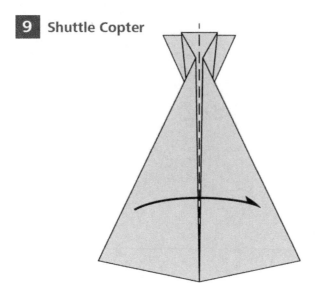

Fold in half and swing about to face you for Step 10.

10 **Shuttle Copter**

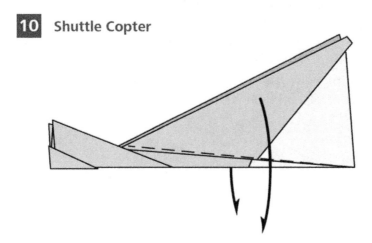

Fold wings down along the angled fuselage.

11 Shuttle Copter

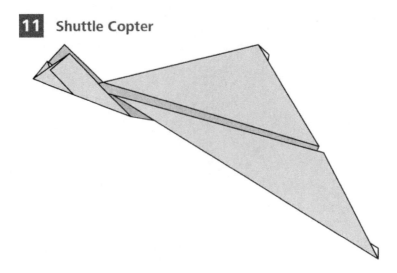

The completed Shuttle Copter. Thrust the craft straight up in the air as hard as you can. This model is best thrown from the top of a building or cliff.

The nose cone is heavy enough to give your throw momentum. When it reaches maximum height from the energy of your throw, it will begin to rotate as gravity takes control, and then gently spin to earth.

Spinner

This craft will catch anyone's eye as it streaks rudely past, spinning on its way to meet its target; ideal for schoolroom antics.

This model has a different basic fold but uses the same folding principle as the Super Looper, where you make creases and collapse the sides together.

1 **Spinner**

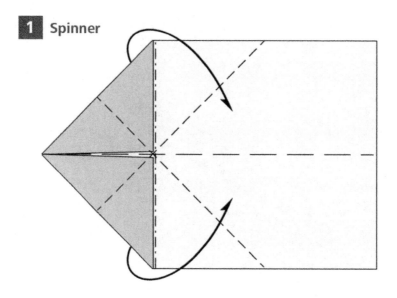

In Step 1, begin with a sheet of paper with the corners folded in as for a regular dart, and having a center crease. Now make diagonal crease-folds and bring the sides together. Step 2 shows this procedure almost done.

2 **Spinner**

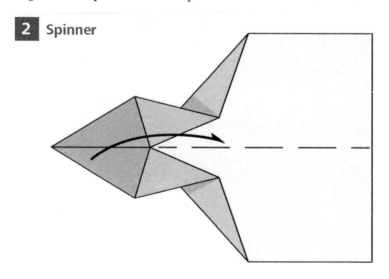

3 Spinner

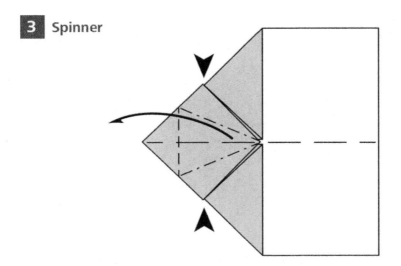

Crease and then open out the triangle section, while pushing in the sides and folding the upper flap to the left.

4 Spinner

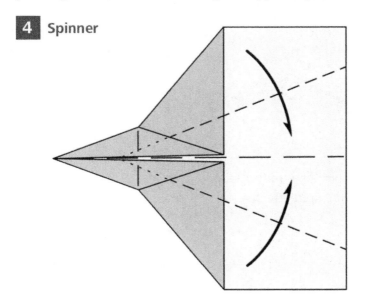

Fold sides in along the dashes indicated, including along the hidden section (dotted lines).

5   Spinner

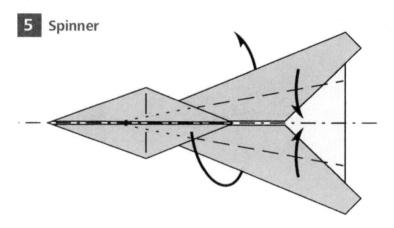

In Step 5, fold sides in again to meet the center crease, and then fold lengthwise in half.

6   Spinner

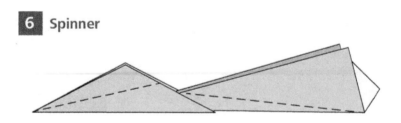

Fold down the wings at opposite angles indicated; this creates the spin effect.

7 **Spinner**

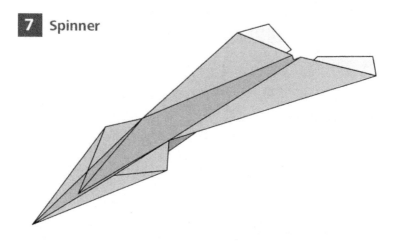

The completed Spinner is ready to annoy! Experiment with this craft by adjusting the wing angles and see how it performs. Throw hard across the school room.

Super Stunt Plane

Similar to the Super Looper but using a slightly different base-fold, this one does lots of acrobatics. Great for throwing in open windy areas such as the park, beach, Congress etc.

1 **Super Stunt Plane**

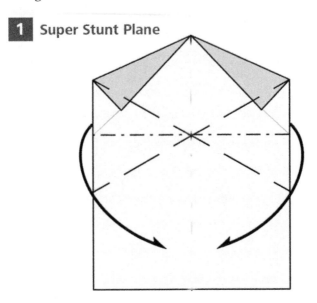

Before you start with Step 1, make the usual center crease, have corners folded in as for a regular dart, unfolded, and then folded to meet the new shallow-angle creases.

In step 1, make the intersecting diagonal creases (shown in the following three steps), plus a horizontal one that also intersects the diagonals. You will then be bringing the sides together to form a slightly different basic fold from the Super Looper.

2 Super Stunt Plane

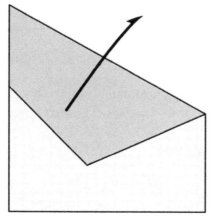

First diagonal (crease fold/unfold).

3 **Super Stunt Plane**

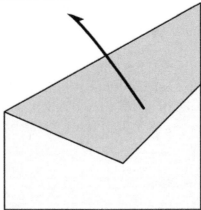

Second (opposite) diagonal (crease fold/unfold).

Where the angles intersect, make a horizontal mountain fold, as you would for the Super Looper base.

4 **Super Stunt Plane**

In Step 4, where the horizontal crease intersects the diagonals, bring in the sides and swing down the top to make our basic fold.

5 Super Stunt Plane

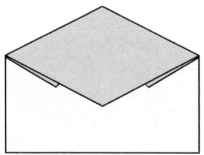

Step 5: Basic fold done! If you are having trouble, please follow these photos (from left to right)...

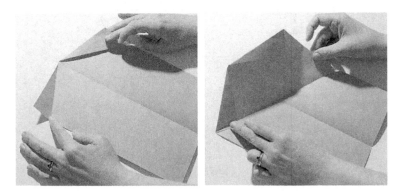

Fold/unfold diagonals and then turn the model over.

Make a horizontal crease where the diagonals intersect.

Push in center, pop up sides, and bring them together.

Flatten the fold.

Done!

6 Super Stunt Plane

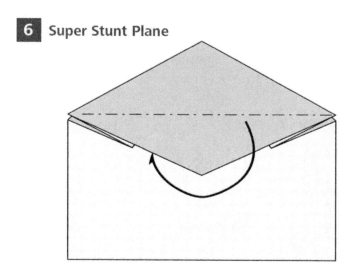

Tuck the lower point in underneath.

7 Super Stunt Plane

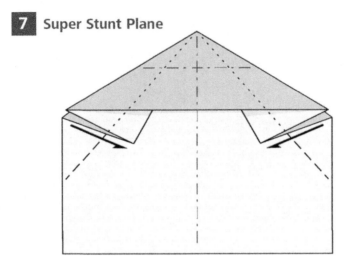

Fold sides under top flap and then fold the nose section behind. Now fold in half behind and swing the paper about to face you as shown in Step 8.

8 Super Stunt Plane

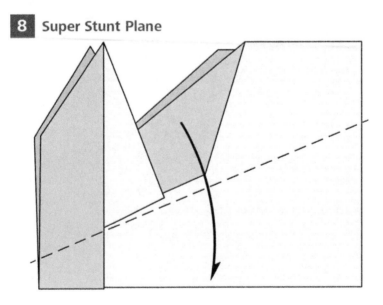

9 Super Stunt Plane

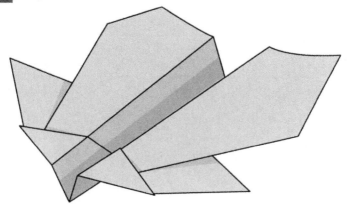

Completed craft; for loops throw vertically with force. For circles throw upwards and away from you with underside facing you. It should return for you to catch.

To catch an upward draft, curl front wing-trails up slightly and then curl up the tail wing trailing edges.

Vertical Takeoff (Jump) Jet

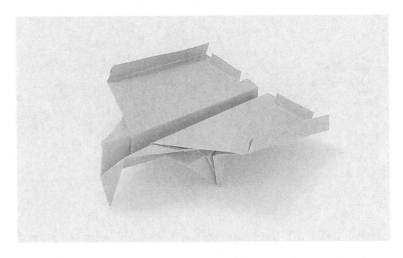

While it doesn't quite look the part of a sleeker jet, this craft does glide and land well on any surface as its steep angle of descent makes it suitable for landing on shorter runways... such as the aircraft carrier in the book, *Paper Boats!*.

This 'take-off' model uses a similar base fold to that shown for the Super Stunt Plane; however you do not need to make shallow-angled folds at the beginning.

Tip: If you add a suitable small drone (propeller underneath the drone's framework) the plane can truly be a 'take-off' aircraft, rather like the old Hawker Siddeley Harrier jump-jets.

1 | Vertical Takeoff Jet

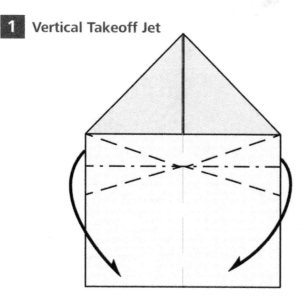

Begin with paper having the corners folded in as for a regular dart. Make creases and complete this special basic fold (shown in Steps 2 – 6).

2 | Vertical Takeoff Jet

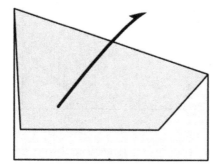

Fold diagonal to the left and then unfold.

3 Vertical Takeoff Jet

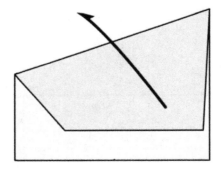

Fold diagonal to the right and then unfold.

4 Vertical Takeoff Jet

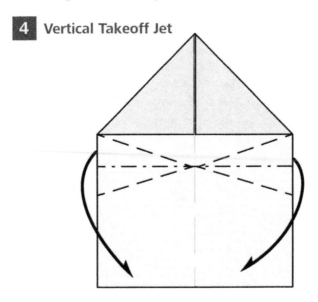

Fold horizontal fold behind, as you have down for other base folds where the diagonals intersect,

Now that you have made your creases, the sides and top should come together easily, just as you have done for the

Super Looper and other models in this book that use similar basic folds...

5 Vertical Takeoff Jet

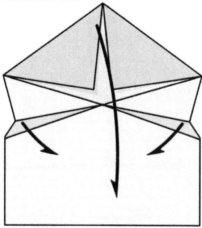

Swing top down and flatten.

6 Vertical Takeoff Jet

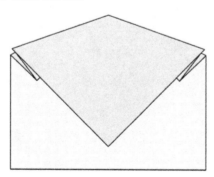

The finished basic fold.

7 Vertical Takeoff Jet

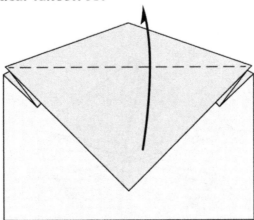

8 Vertical Takeoff Jet

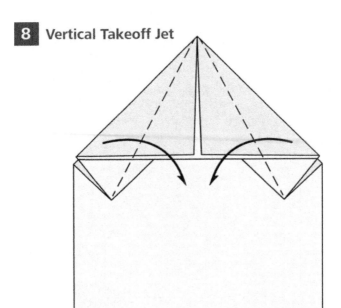

9 Vertical Takeoff Jet

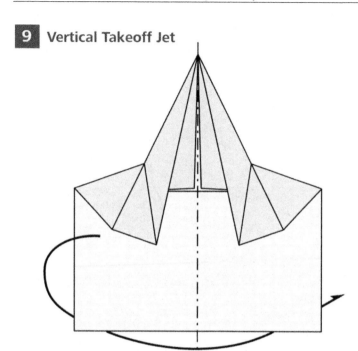

10 Vertical Takeoff Jet

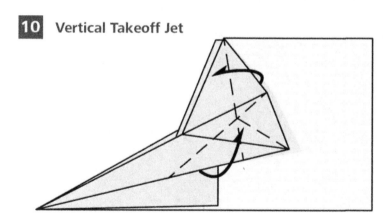

In Step 10, make the creases and pinch the edges together to form a rabbit/bunny ear; this will become our undercarriage. The next steps show cutaways of the undercarriage folds in detail.

11 **Vertical Takeoff Jet**

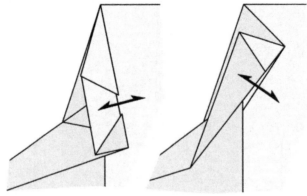

Make crease folds, and then pinch the sides together to make the rabbit ears.

12 **Vertical Takeoff Jet**

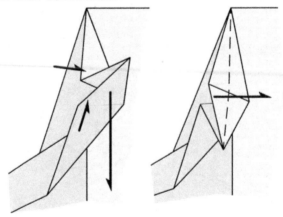

In Step 12, swing down the rabbit ear and flatten. Next, fold upper flap to the right for reinforcement.

13 Vertical Takeoff Jet

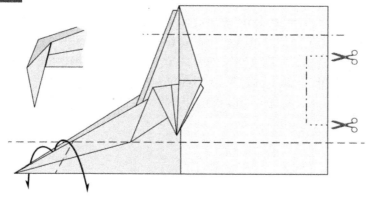

Your undercarriage will look like this.

Fold the nose: reverse-fold (inside out) to make a 90 degree-angle nose landing leg.

Finally, fold wings, fins, and add tail lift.

14 Vertical Takeoff Jet

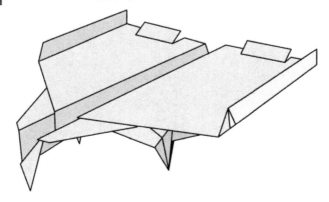

The completed jet; throw horizontally with a gentle motion. Do not launch at high angles as it will stall.

Modification experiment

For a sleeker-looking version, it's possible to experiment with the wing span by doing a clever inverse fold at the top section of the undercarriage (before making the wing fins) and angling back the wing edge to the trailing wing tips. I'll leave the experimentation up to you, but here is my first attempt…

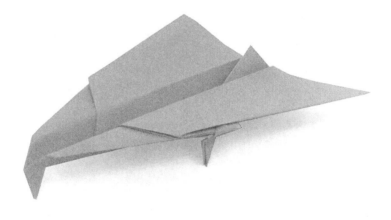

Modified jet

Concorde

This graceful craft can once again streak across the skies and it's relatively easy to make, and noise-free! This model uses the same basic fold as the Vertical Take-off Jet.

1 Concorde

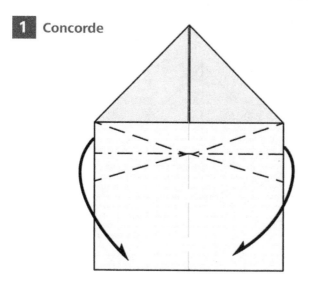

Make the same basic fold as the Vertical Takeoff Jet (Steps 2 – 6).

2 Concorde

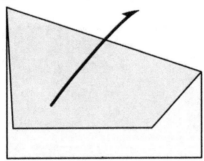

3 Concorde

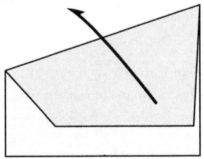

4 Concorde

Creases done; now bring the sides together – you should be used to this by now :)

5 Concorde

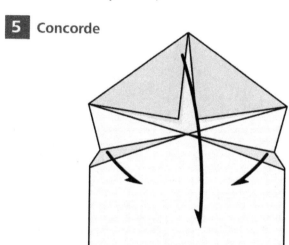

6 Concorde

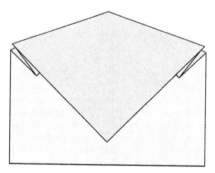

The finished basic fold. Note: the lower point may touch the bottom edge depending on what size paper you use (typical for A4).

7 Concorde

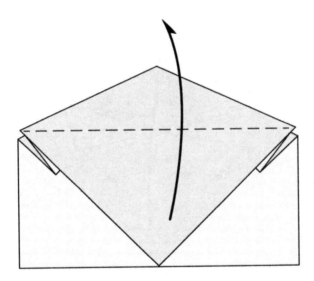

8 Concorde

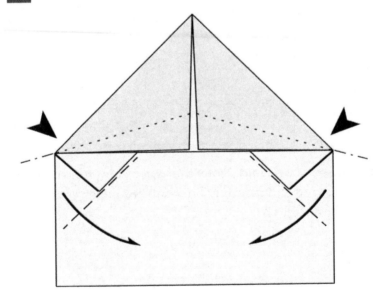

In Step 8, inverse-fold the right and left lower flap edges by opening out the fold and pushing the sides inwards.

Step 9 shows the right side fold half-complete.

9 Concorde

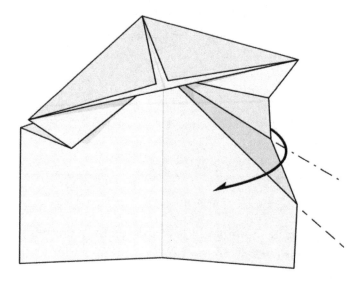

Right-side almost done; repeat for the left and then flatten the fold.

10 **Concorde**

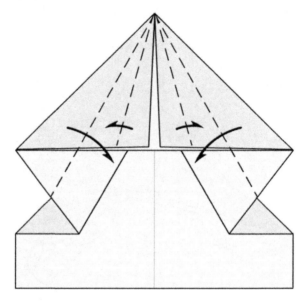

As you fold the outer sides inwards to make wing edges, fold the inner flaps (closer to the center) underneath.

11 **Concorde**

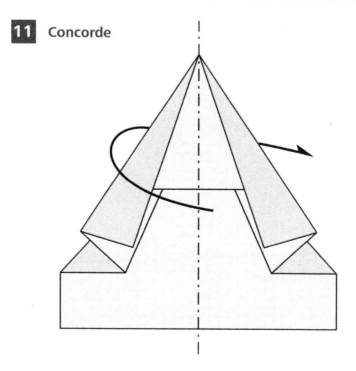

Fold in half behind.

12 Concorde

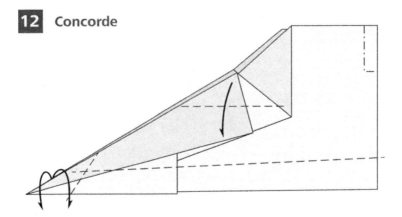

Crease and open out the nose section, and reverse the fold (making it inside out).

Next, fold down the simple landing gear, fold down wings at a shallow angle, and then add tail lift for stability (snip for rear lift).

13 Concorde

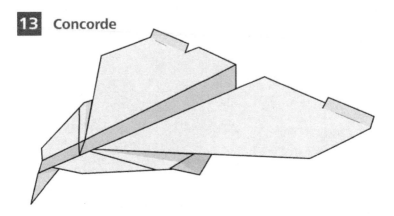

The completed Concorde; throw horizontally with a gentle forward motion. It will glide well before landing gracefully. There is a video of this on Dwight's **Paper Plane Lab** YouTube channel.

You could give the aircraft a vertical tail by inverse-folding the end of the fuselage; crease-fold at an angle and then push in to make the tail wing (as shown in the modified Vertical Takeoff Jet photo). Note that you may have a stability issue which is why I don't include it in the instructions, but it will look cool :)

The following photo shows the Concorde parked in The Hangar (from *The Best Advanced Paper Aircraft Book 3*).

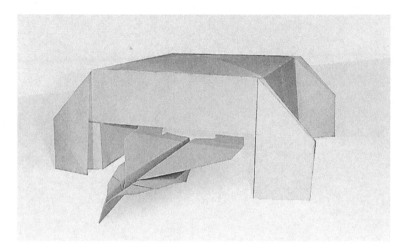

Printed in Great Britain
by Amazon

17889879R00058